KICK A$$

SMALL TALK

HOW TO SAY SH*T TO ANYONE, ANYWHERE

Quarto

This edition published in 2025 by Chartwell Books,
an imprint of The Quarto Group
142 West 36th Street, 4th Floor
New York, NY 10018 USA
T (212) 779-4972
www.Quarto.com

10 9 8 7 6 5 4 3 2 1

Chartwell titles are also available at discount for retail, wholesale, promotional, and bulk purchase. For details, contact the Special Sales Manager by email at specialsales@quarto.com or by mail at The Quarto Group, Attn: Special Sales Manager, 100 Cummings Center Suite 265D, Beverly, MA 01915, USA.

ISBN: 978-0-7858-4646-8

Publisher: Wendy Friedman
Publishing Director: Meredith Mennitt
Cover Designer: Sue Boylan
Designer: Angelika Piwowarczyk

Printed in China

KICK A$$ SMALL TALK

HOW TO SAY SH*T TO ANYONE, ANYWHERE

chartwell
books

CONTENTS

Introduction

WHAT'S EVERYONE TALKING ABOUT?

HUMANS ARE SOCIAL CREATURES. WE LIVE IN COMMUNITIES AND HAVE WORKED TOGETHER FOR CENTURIES TO SURVIVE AND THRIVE IN THIS WORLD. THESE SOCIAL BONDS AND COMMUNITIES ARE BUILT THROUGH COMMUNICATION. WHILE WE MAY NOT BE BEST FRIENDS WITH EVERYONE, IT'S HARD TO CREATE A LIFE WITH TOTAL STRANGERS.

Though we are still social creatures, the world that we live in has become less sociable over the years. With our social lives becoming increasingly digital, combined with multiple isolating global events such as war, illness, and alienating politics, we've become less willing to engage with each other. It's easier to look at our phones than talk to our Uber drivers. We may feel nervous ordering at the deli, unsure if we are doing it "correctly." We may even ignore our coworkers because we're worried about embarrassing ourselves or saying something wrong. As our world comes to feel less friendly and communicative, we become more isolated. What's the solution to this?

SMALL TALK!

As unpopular an answer as this might be, if you picked up this book, you knew it would be the solution. Small talk has gotten a bad reputation and people tend to have some BIG feelings about it—

including disdain, discomfort, and even embarrassment. It's easy to write off small talk as trivial: why talk about the weather when you have better things to do? However, small talk isn't as basic as that. In fact, learning to be fluent in small talk can have huge benefits, such as:

BUILDING CONFIDENCE: Studies have shown that being able to strike up a conversation with someone can boost your mental health and make you feel more confident, both in social situations and about yourself in general. If you can talk to someone without panicking, there's nothing you can't achieve.

STRENGTHENING CONNECTIONS: Remember, humans are social creatures. While it might be easier to text people or send memes, it's not the same as making an in-person connection. You tend to gain more opportunities by talking to someone than you would by being a faceless, voiceless avatar on the screen. For example, talking to a fellow parent at your child's school could lead to signing your child up for enriching after-school programs. Talking to people on your commute can give you restaurant recommendations. All these things can make your life richer.

GAINING SURVIVAL SKILLS: While this may seem a little dramatic, small talk is a survival skill in our social world. Studies have shown that being able to make small talk with your doctor could affect the care and attention you receive. Your daily banter with the

person in Human Resources may spare you from a round of layoffs. While this may not be fair, never underestimate what the right word can do for you.

FUN FACT:
A British poll revealed that, with conversations lasting less than three minutes, Britons spend about four and a half months of their lives chatting about the weather. Half of the respondents said it's their go-to small-talk topic, one-third said they're happy to talk weather with strangers, and forty percent said they'll turn to the weather to fill silences with a coworker.

IMPROVING YOUR OUTLOOK ON LIFE: Let's face it, it's easy to become jaded in our world today. Online, we encounter trolls, rants, and people with the worst opinions and motivations. It's hard not to think everyone is like that. However, when we log off and *actually talk* to each other, we can realize that we're not as divided as we thought. We don't have to talk out *everything*—life is not a debate meeting—but gaining some common ground on simple topics can help us believe the world isn't such a dark place. While we may seem more divided and isolated than ever, a simple conversation can change everything.

Welcome to Kick A$$ Small Talk

Kick A$$ Small Talk is here to help you navigate the world of micro-interactions. While we may consider small talk boring or draining, we also cannot build a relationship by telling a stranger our life story at first glance, or by talking our seatmate's ear off about our opinion on aliens during a 12-hour flight. This book can help you find a happy medium between deep talks and polite chatting. Whether you have trouble reading social cues, have social anxiety, or feel a little rusty on the art of making conversation, this book is here to guide you into strengthening your communication muscles through:

- SKILL-BUILDING EXERCISES TO GET YOU OUT OF YOUR COMFORT ZONE;
- WRITING PROMPTS TO HELP YOU ANALYZE THE WAY YOU COMMUNICATE;
- REFLECTIVE QUESTIONS TO HELP YOU LEARN AND GROW.

Even if you don't consider yourself an extrovert or born with the gift of gab, you can be a successful communicator. Remember, communication is a skill like anything else. While some people may be naturally better at it, it is still something that can be learned.

Kick A$$ Small Talk is a workbook that is part advice guide and part cheerleader to give you tips and tricks on how to talk your way through any situation: from networking events to moving to a new place. Whether you struggle to make chitchat with your distant relatives, or feel like you have nothing interesting to say, this book can help you find your voice. With more than 100 writing prompts and thoughtful exercises, this book will have you faking it till you make it, one conversation at a time.

Each chapter also features reflection questions, dos and don'ts, challenges, and mantras to help you become a better communicator. Topics include:

- WHAT TYPE OF COMMUNICATOR ARE YOU?
- MICRO-INTERACTIONS
- SMALL TALK WITH FAMILY
- SMALL TALK AND RELATIONSHIPS
- SMALL TALK IN PROFESSIONAL SITUATIONS
- WRITTEN COMMUNICATION (YES, WRITTEN SMALL TALK IS JUST AS IMPORTANT AS VERBAL!)

The Stages of Small Talk

Contrary to popular belief (or what we see in the movies), small talk doesn't just happen. Sure, you *could* just walk up to a stranger on the street and start gabbing with them, but if you could do that, why are you reading this book? For a lot of us, though, that's a pretty terrifying thought. The good news is that most small talk happens in stages, which will help build up your confidence and your connections with others. Now, not all small talk will lead to deep conversation, but these are the types of conversation, from small to large, that you'll move through in your life:

MICRO:
Interactions you have daily; very brief, usually do not go past "hello" or "good morning." Think: mailman, neighbors, the cashier at the grocery store.

QUICK CHATS:
Brief chats as you go about your daily life; short conversation while still moving on. Think: parents at the drop-off line, barista at the coffee shop, neighbors walking their dog.

SMALL TALK:
Short conversation that usually takes a few minutes; simple topics like the weather or general interest; typically not too personal.

DEEP CONVERSATION:
Usually with people you've known for a long time (but not always); usually lasts for a longer period of time; can cover personal and complex topics.

How to Use This Book

Kick A$$ Small Talk wants you to take it one word at a time, knowing you can build this skill with patience and practice. Since everyone has different communication needs, this book allows you to skip around chapters and focus on different areas, depending on what your needs are.

We'll start, however, with understanding what type of communicator you are and the challenges and goals you have. Each chapter will then feature tips and tricks on how to successfully make small talk in different situations. The prompts, exercises, topic suggestions, and reflection questions are here to help pull you out of your comfort zone, whether that's going on a "conversation scavenger hunt" or introducing yourself to people in your community. Look for conversation bubbles throughout to help you along the way. By the end, you should be confident and capable of starting and holding any conversation without fear.

So let's get yapping!

Small Talk Tip:

When used sparingly, filler words like "um" and "ah," and hedge words like "just" or "actually," can be useful in conversation. They can aid in diplomacy, hold your place to avoid interruption, or help you break into a conversation (so long as you're not cutting someone off). It's when they're used excessively that they can detract from your credibility or authority.

"Good conversation is as stimulating as black coffee, and just as hard to sleep after."

ANNE MORROW LINDBERGH

CHAPTER 1

WHAT TYPE OF COMMUNICATOR ARE YOU?

Not all small talk is created equal. Most communication is dependent on a variety of factors including setting, mood, personal comfort level, topics, ability to read social cues, and whom we're communicating with, among other things. By reading this book, you are acknowledging that your small talk skills could use some improvement, but in what way? Are you loud and vibrant with your best friends but avoid giving your coffee order to the barista? Can you spill your deepest secrets to a cashier but are reluctant to talk about your personal life in front of your family? Do you talk about anything and nothing with your partner but are shy around your coworkers because your mind goes blank?

All these situations are common. Sometimes it's easier to talk to a stranger than to people we know, and sometimes it's easier to relax and cut loose around the people who make us feel comfortable. One person's comfort zone is another person's anxiety nightmare. Before we learn the subtle art of making small talk, it's important to understand your own feelings about it, as well as your strengths and weaknesses.

Do you consider yourself to be an introvert or an extrovert? Explain why you feel like this.

How comfortable do you feel talking to new people?

What is more comfortable for you: starting or responding to a conversation? Why do you feel like this?

What intimidates you the most about small talk? What do you struggle with?

What's driving you to get better at small talk?

Defining Your Communication Strengths and Weaknesses

Everyone has strengths and weaknesses when it comes to communication. What may come easy to you can be a struggle for someone else. Small talk is only one type of communication, and even though you may feel like you don't thrive with this type of communication, you may have stronger skills in other forms, like actively listening or writing solid grant proposals; these skills can help you develop your small talk muscles. To do this, you need to understand what type of communicator you are.

Below, check off everything you relate to. This isn't a personality test—you won't be scored on anything. This list is to help you see what areas of communication you feel most comfortable with to help you navigate the world of small talk.

- ☐ I feel I can express myself better in writing than in person.
- ☐ I feel more comfortable talking to a large group than one-on-one.
- ☐ I have a difficult time coming up with interesting conversation topics.
- ☐ I have a hard time focusing on what someone is trying to tell me, especially when I feel overstimulated.
- ☐ My close friends say I'm very chatty, but I clam up with people I don't know.
- ☐ It takes me a long time to warm up to people.
- ☐ I can read between the lines when people are talking.
- ☐ I tend to take what people tell me at face value.
- ☐ I have a hard time knowing when a conversation is over.
- ☐ I have a hard time understanding social cues or "reading a room."
- ☐ I'd rather start a conversation than be approached.
- ☐ I am comfortable with long silences.
- ☐ I notice everything but say very little.
- ☐ I am highly intuitive.

- ☐ People tend to approach me for conversation, despite me not initiating it.
- ☐ I prefer people to text me than call me.
- ☐ I prefer people to call me, as texting leads to miscommunication.
- ☐ I can easily talk for hours about subjects I am interested in/knowledgeable about.
- ☐ I am a better listener than a speaker.
- ☐ I tend to reply to conversations with simple or one-word answers.
- ☐ I have been known to overshare with strangers.
- ☐ I tend to be very private with information about myself or my feelings.
- ☐ I feel anxious in social situations.
- ☐ I tend to overanalyze the conversations long after they are over.
- ☐ I need to think about my actions and responses thoroughly before acting or speaking.
- ☐ I tend to speak off the cuff, without thinking it through.
- ☐ How talkative I am depends on my mood.
- ☐ I am a social butterfly in certain settings, a wallflower in others.
- ☐ I have a hard time communicating in a public setting.

After checking things off the list, do you notice any patterns? Write your observations.

Is there a communication strength or weakness you have that wasn't listed in the checklist? Write it here.

How do you think you can use your communication strengths and even your weaknesses to improve your small talk skills?

The Setting of Small Talk

As they say in real estate, it's all about location, location, location. The same can be said about small talk. Sometimes, small talk thrives in certain areas, like at a baseball game or the office break room, and flounder in other places, like at orientation or when the plumber comes to work at your house. There are plenty of factors that make small talk happen: the location, the mood, the topics, and the people you are talking to. It takes two to have a conversation, after all. In this section, think about your ideal small talk settings and conversations you've had before to understand where you flourish, and what you need to work on.

What was the best or most memorable conversation you ever had? What was it about? Who was it with? Did small talk lead up to it?

What was the most awkward conversation you ever had? What happened that made it so uncomfortable? What would you do differently now?

Who is the person you feel most comfortable talking to? Why are they so easy to talk to?

Who in your life is the hardest to talk to? Why do you think that is?

Think about some things you usually do in public settings that involve other people, like standing in line or sitting in a rideshare. Do you tend to start conversation, engage in conversation, or avoid it?

Being able to read a room can make or break most small talk. Do you have trouble reading social cues? If so, what do you miss most often?

What is your ideal conversation setting?

What is your nightmare conversation setting?

Small Talk = Big Goals

Of course, the hope is that by reading this book you feel more confident in engaging in small talk and can hold your own in any conversation. However, there are many reasons to want to improve at small talk, and that improvement looks different for everyone—whether you wish to make friends in a new city, overcome social anxiety, or put yourself back into the world after a long period of being closed off from others. It's one thing to want to improve your skills, but setting goals can give you the motivation you need to do it. These goals won't be achieved overnight, but they give you something to work towards during this journey. Use the following pages to create goals for one month, six months, and one year in the future. These can be as simple as making conversation at a parenting group or something big like making a new friend through small talk. To help inspire your goals, review your answers to the checklist on page 18, and you can also look through the exercises in this book for ideas.

One-Month Goals

Write out at least three goals you wish to achieve by the end of the month. These don't have to be big goals. Start with small ones that are easy to manage, like starting a conversation with your new neighbor or calling someone instead of texting. Keep it simple.

GOAL 1

I will complete this goal by: ___/___/___

....

....

....

GOAL 2

I will complete this goal by: ___/___/___

....

....

....

GOAL 3

I will complete this goal by: ___/___/___

....

....

....

Six-Month Goals

Now that you have some momentum going, think about where you want to be in six months. Set three goals you wish to achieve during that time. It can be in any area of your life, like inviting the neighbor to go on a walk around the neighborhood or going on a first date. If it feels overwhelming, you can gain inspiration from the exercises and challenges in the book, like the Small Talk Scavenger Hunt on page 92.

GOAL 1

I will complete this goal by: ___/___/___

....

....

....

GOAL 2

I will complete this goal by: ___/___/___

....

....

....

GOAL 3

I will complete this goal by: ___/___/___

....

....

....

One-Year Goals

A lot can happen in a year! Think about where you are and where you want to be. Set three goals you wish to achieve over the course of a year when you are a more experienced and confident speaker, like having the confidence to change jobs or making friends with people in your building.

GOAL 1

I will complete this goal by: ___/___/___

....

....

....

GOAL 2

I will complete this goal by: ___/___/___

....

....

....

GOAL 3

I will complete this goal by: ___/___/___

....

....

....

A NOTE ON SAFETY: Throughout this book, we'll be encouraging you to get out of your comfort zone and talk to people, including total strangers. However, it's important to always put your safety first; if someone or a situation is making you feel uncomfortable, it's always okay to leave. Remember to use your best judgment whether someone is okay to approach—or if you should just leave them be.

“A conversation is so much more than words: a conversation is eyes, smiles, the silences between words.”

ANNIKA THOR

CHAPTER 2

CONVERSATION BASICS

One of the most intimidating aspects of small talk is the beginning. How does one start a conversation? This question seems easy, as we've all talked to people before, and we've all made small talk before. However, the basics of conversation can be a little nerve-wracking, especially if we've been out of practice or unsure of what to say to the person standing in front of us. In this chapter, we'll be getting down to the basics of small talk to help you on your conversation journey.

Before we begin, let's do a brief check-in:

How well do you know the basics of small talk?

DO PEOPLE STILL SAY "HI"?	○	○	○	○	○	○	○	○	○	○	I MAKE GOOD SMALL TALK
	1	2	3	4	5	6	7	8	9	10	

Why do you feel this way?

....

....

....

....

....

....

What are you hoping to improve on?

....

....

....

....

....

....

The Four Steps of Small Talk

While making even basic small talk can seem intimidating or overwhelming, it actually can be broken down into four steps. These steps can help you be successful in any situation where small talk might be necessary.

FUN FACT:
People spend about 60 percent of a conversation talking about themselves. According to research using functional magnetic resonance imaging, it feels good to do so!

STEP 1: BE PRESENT

In our modern world, it's easy to get distracted by our phones—and we often use them to avoid making small talk. However, if you want to make good conversation, you need to put away your phone and any other distractions and be in the moment to fully engage with the person you wish to talk to.

People will be more willing to interact with you if you put in the effort to be present. For example, when someone is talking to you on a bus, this would mean not keeping your finger on the page of the magazine you're hoping to return to or not holding one earbud in your hand, showing you're literally only half listening. Make an effort, say hi, and let the conversation begin. Remember, it's a social experience; soak it in.

STEP 2: ASK OPEN-ENDED QUESTIONS

Once we get through the basic conversation openers of "hello" or "good morning," it's good to start with a question. These questions should be fairly basic and open ended (not answerable with "yes" or "no"); you don't want to get too personal with someone you don't know very well as it could be awkward. We'll go over question suggestions later in the chapter, but some good questions to start with are:

HOW ARE YOU TODAY?

WHAT DO YOU DO FOR WORK?

WHAT DID YOU THINK OF TODAY'S MEETING/LECTURE?

Of course, these questions will depend on the context of your situation and conversation partner. Try to keep the conversation light and steer clear of trying to open a conversation with gossip or hyper-specific questions, as they can hinder the conversation rather than develop it. The beauty of using open-ended questions is that it creates room to grow into a full conversation.

STEP 3: LISTEN

While we'll be spending a great deal of time on the speaking aspect of small talk, listening is just as important. Being an active listener is an essential skill we often take for granted. No one wants to be in a conversation where they don't feel heard; it can be discouraging and ends the conversation in a lull. Here are some tips on how to be an active listener:

- MAKE EYE CONTACT (BUT DON'T STARE).
- NOD OR SHAKE YOUR HEAD AT WHAT THE OTHER PERSON IS SAYING.
- DON'T LOOK AT YOUR PHONE/WATCH OR LOOK AROUND THE ROOM.

- WAIT UNTIL THE PERSON IS DONE TALKING BEFORE SPEAKING.
- IF YOU ARE ENGAGING IN SMALL TALK ON THE PHONE, GIVE ENCOURAGING SOUNDS LIKE "YES" OR "MMHMM."

By listening, we can get to know the person better, come up with replies and different questions, and keep the small talk going.

STEP 4: RESPOND WITH ENTHUSIASM

Have you ever had a conversation where someone asks you a question, you give a thoughtful answer, and they give you a one-word response? It's disheartening and can leave a person feeling off-balance in the conversation. When making small talk, you never want to feel like you are wasting someone's time or make them feel like you are not interested in what they have to say.

Small talk is about having fun and learning more about another person, so respond with attention and enthusiasm. Put yourself fully into the conversation. Whether you're giving your opinion about the topic, sharing your experience, or asking a follow-up question, put yourself into the conversation to develop it. When all else fails, say, "That's so interesting. Can you tell me more?"

Reflection Questions

Which part of the Four Steps of Small Talk comes easily to you? What might you need to improve on?

How can you use the Four Steps of Small Talk in your next conversation? Come up with an action plan for yourself, even hypothetically.

When to Make Conversation

Now that we have the basics down, it's time to go over how to start a conversation, which might be an intimidating task. Now, we're not going to ask you to walk up to a person on the street and make them talk to you (yet), but there are many situations where you're encouraged to make the first move in conversation: at work, in class, at networking events, on business calls, etc. There are also places and situations where you have the opportunity to make the first move, like a school drop-off, with your seatmate on a flight or train, or when a maintenance person comes to do repairs. In these situations, it can be harder to tell when someone wants to make conversation—or whether you should.

Here are some ways to tell when it is okay to make conversation with someone:

- THEY MAKE EYE CONTACT WITH YOU AND SMILE.
- THEY HAVE AN OPEN POSTURE (HEAD UP, SHOULDERS BACK).
- THEY ARE BY THEMSELVES OR NOT ENGAGED IN CONVERSATION WITH OTHERS.
- THEY ARE TURNED TOWARDS YOU.
- THEIR VOICE IS FRIENDLY.
- THERE IS A LULL IN ACTIVITY (BEFORE CLASS BEGINS, AFTER A WORK MEETING, BEFORE THE PLANE TAKES OFF, WAITING FOR A PLAY TO BEGIN, TIMEOUT BETWEEN QUARTERS, ETC.).

Psst... These are also things *you* can do to let people know you are open to engaging in conversation.

Small Talk Tip:

It's important to remember that *everyone* is nervous about making small talk, and most people will be relieved that you made the first move. So have fun with it!

When Not to Make Conversation

When you're nervous about making small talk, you may use *anything* as an excuse to avoid it. While most people welcome small talk (even though it scares us), here are some examples of when making small talk isn't advised.

- THEY ARE ACTIVELY AVOIDING YOUR GAZE.
- THEY HAVE A CLOSED POSTURE (ARMS CROSSED, HEAD DOWN).
- THEY ARE ON THEIR PHONE OR ARE TALKING TO SOMEONE ELSE.
- THEY ARE TURNED AWAY FROM YOU.
- IT'S A BUSY TIME (DURING A MEETING, THEY'RE DOING THEIR JOB, PEOPLE ARE RUSHING AROUND, THE GAME HAS STARTED, ETC.).

If you have trouble understanding body language or social cues, it may take you longer to learn when someone is open to small talk. Don't be afraid to make the first move and approach someone. Even if that person is not open to talking, as long as you are friendly and leave them alone as soon as you understand they are not interested, it won't be a completely embarrassing situation but a learning experience. Try not to take it personally.

SMALL TALK CHALLENGE

Go to a place you attend frequently that has people you see often (work, fitness class, coffeeshop, etc.) and notice their body language. How many people seemed open to small talk and how many people seemed closed off? Write down what you observed below. Bonus points if you make small talk with someone who seemed open to it!

Rate how it went:

Topics and Responses to Remember

Okay, so we now know how to approach someone for small talk and the basic formula for it, but here's the biggest question: What do you say? It's easy to draw a blank, especially if you're nervous. Fortunately, to help ease some anxiety, you can prepare yourself by having some topics and responses on memory-redial to help you kick the conversation off *and* keep it going.

SMALL TALK TOPIC IDEAS

In the 1964 film *My Fair Lady*, Professor Henry Higgins (played by Rex Harrison) tells his student, Eliza Doolittle (played by Audrey Hepburn), that when mingling with London's high society she should stick to two topics: the weather and everyone's health. These were considered to be polite conversation topics, as they don't stir up passion or bring out different opinions, like politics. However, limiting yourself to only two topics can get real boring real fast. Plus, talking about health can be a tricky subject matter, especially if someone has been going through a health challenge that you didn't realize. To widen your conversational horizons, here is a list of topics that are typically drama free and can create an interesting conversation.

> ***Small Talk Tip:***
>
> **While these topics are good for most general audiences, please use your best judgment, as something that would seem tame to one person may set off another.**

WORK:

- WHEN DID YOU FIRST START WORKING HERE?
- WHAT DO YOU LIKE MOST ABOUT YOUR JOB?
- WHAT'S THE BEST CAREER ADVICE YOU RECEIVED?
- WHAT ARE SOME OF YOUR CAREER GOALS?
- WHAT GOT YOU INTERESTED IN WORKING IN THIS PROFESSION?

ENTERTAINMENT:

- I'M LOOKING TO GET BACK INTO READING. WHAT BOOKS WOULD YOU RECOMMEND?
- I JUST FINISHED [INSERT SHOW]. WHAT HAVE YOU BEEN WATCHING LATELY?
- I FEEL LIKE I'M ALWAYS ON TIKTOK. WHAT'S ON YOUR *FOR YOU* PAGE?
- I JUST GOT [INSERT STREAMING SERVICE]. WHAT DO YOU RECOMMEND I START WITH?
- WHAT ARE YOU CURRENTLY LISTENING TO?

LOCAL ATTRACTIONS/ TRAVEL:

- DO YOU HAVE ANY VACATION PLANS COMING UP?
- WHAT IS YOUR FAVORITE THING TO DO IN TOWN?
- DID YOU HEAR ABOUT THE NEW [RESTAURANT/STORE/EVENT] COMING UP? ARE YOU EXCITED ABOUT IT?
- WHAT IS YOUR DREAM VACATION?
- WHAT ARE THE TOP THREE SONGS ON YOUR ROAD-TRIP PLAYLIST?

FOOD:

- I'M NEW IN TOWN. WHAT IS YOUR GO-TO RESTAURANT AROUND HERE?
- HAVE YOU TRIED THE NEW [INSERT RESTAURANT NAME]? IS IT GOOD?
- WHAT IS YOUR GO-TO TAKEOUT ORDER?
- DO YOU COOK? WHAT IS YOUR SIGNATURE DISH?
- IF YOU COULD EAT ONE THING FOR THE REST OF YOUR LIFE, WHAT WOULD IT BE?

(AND, WHEN IN DOUBT, YOU CAN ALWAYS TALK ABOUT THE WEATHER.)

Small Talk Tip:

To maintain confidence, instead of interrupting a conversation or turning the topic with "I'm sorry, but..." try "Thank you..." Instead of "I think that..." try "In my experience..."

RESPONSES TO REMEMBER

So you have someone chatting with you, yay! Now it's time to respond. If you aren't sure what to say to someone, here are some ideas to keep in your back pocket when you're feeling stuck. Again, use your best judgment for how these responses fit in with your conversation.

AND THEN WHAT HAPPENED?

THAT SOUNDS SO COOL/ INTERESTING.

THAT REMINDS ME WHEN [SHARE A TIME SOMETHING SIMILAR HAPPENED].

I REMEMBER WHEN...

And, when in doubt, remember to smile and nod.

SMALL TALK CHALLENGE

Pick out a couple sample topics and questions and try them out on someone you see during the day. Use the space below to write down what you used and how it went.

Rate how it went:

Ending the Conversation

All good things must come to an end, and small talk is no different. While small talk *could* lead to deep conversation, sometimes you just need to end it so you can get on with your day. But for anyone who has been in a long conversation where people are just not done talking or been stuck in a conversation going nowhere, it can feel tricky to end it without feeling rude or awkward. Fortunately, there are some ways to smoothly transition out of a conversation while saving face.

The easiest way to end a conversation is by letting the other person know that you need to leave and do other things. Some examples to use are:

- "IT'S BEEN SO NICE TALKING TO YOU, BUT I NEED TO CATCH UP ON SOME WORK."
- "EXCUSE ME, I HAVE TO HEAD OUT."
- "IT WAS SO GOOD TO SEE YOU! TAKE CARE."
- "THAT'S SO INTERESTING, AND I'D LOVE TO HEAR MORE. HOWEVER, I REALLY NEED TO GET BACK TO MY STUDIES."
- "SEE YOU LATER!"

There's no shame in ending a conversation. Just make sure you're firm and showing body language that indicates that you're ready to leave: turning away from them, packing up your stuff, crossing your arms, etc. This is always a good way to tell if someone is ready to leave the conversation.

Small Talk Script

Here's an example of basic small talk between Peggy and Angela, who go to the same gym. Peggy approaches Angela after spin class.

PEGGY: WOW! THAT CLASS WAS INTENSE.
WHAT DID YOU THINK OF IT?

ANGELA: I KNOW! I DIDN'T THINK I WAS GOING TO KEEP UP
AFTER MISSING THE LAST THREE CLASSES FOR VACATION.

I THOUGHT I HADN'T SEEN YOU IN A WHILE.
WHERE DID YOU TRAVEL TO?

I WENT TO PARIS! IT'S BEEN A
DREAM OF MINE SINCE I WAS A KID.

ME TOO! PARIS AND AMSTERDAM ARE ON MY BUCKET LIST.
I'M PLANNING ON GOING TO FRANCE NEXT SPRING.

YOU WILL LOVE IT! THERE'S SO MUCH TO DO AND THE FOOD IS AMAZING! I'LL GIVE YOU SOME RECOMMENDATIONS. THERE'S A LITTLE PASTRY SHOP I CAN'T STOP THINKING ABOUT.

I'D LOVE THAT! I'M PEGGY BY THE WAY.

I'M ANGELA. IT'S NICE TO TALK TO YOU.

SAME HERE. I'LL SEE YOU NEXT TIME!

Small Talk Mantras

If you're still anxious about making small talk, here are some mantras to repeat to yourself to both motivate and relax you.

I CAN DEVELOP A BETTER VERSION OF MYSELF BY TAKING ACTION.

EVERY JOURNEY BEGINS WITH A SINGLE STEP.

EVERYONE LIKES ME UNTIL PROVEN OTHERWISE.

I AM A LIKABLE AND INTERESTING PERSON.

EVERY TIME I AM BRAVE, I AM ONE STEP CLOSER TO BEING MY TRUE SELF.

What are some mantras you can say to yourself to build confidence? Write them here.

....

....

....

....

CHAPTER CHALLENGE

Try everything you learned in this chapter by approaching someone you see daily, or at least frequently, but have not talked to before, and make small talk from start to finish. Write about how it went and include both highlights and things you could improve on for the next conversation.

Rate how it went:

CHAPTER CHALLENGE

Practice makes perfect! If you're a little nervous about making small talk with someone you don't know, ask a close friend or loved one to role-play a short conversation to help you practice. When you are finished, have your friend give you feedback and write it below.

Rate how it went:

Reflection Questions

What is one piece of advice you will be taking away from this chapter? Write about how it has helped you or will help you.

Do you feel more confident about making small talk now? Write about why or why not.

USE THIS SPACE TO WRITE DOWN CONVERSATIONS YOU HAVE, JOURNAL HOW YOU'RE FEELING, OR HOW THIS CHAPTER HELPED YOU GET CLOSER TO YOUR GOALS. WHEN IN DOUBT, WRITE IT OUT!

"Conversation doesn't have to lead to consensus about anything, especially not values; it's enough that it helps people get used to one another."

KWAME ANTHONY APPIAH

CHAPTER 3

MICRO-INTERACTIONS

We interact with people often, whether we see them for a moment or as a fixture of our daily lives. Even if we aren't having long conversations with others, we are having several quick ones throughout the day. These are called micro-interactions. Micro-interactions are quick conversations with people (usually strangers) that you encounter throughout your day and consist of little more than a few words. Micro-interactions include:

- THE BARISTA AT YOUR COFFEESHOP
- THE DRIVER OF YOUR RIDESHARE
- PEOPLE YOU PASS WALKING DOWN THE STREET
- PEOPLE WHO WORK IN YOUR OFFICE BUILDING
- PEOPLE WHO COMMENT ON YOUR SOCIAL MEDIA POSTS
- PEOPLE IN RESTAURANTS (INCLUDING THE STAFF)
- AND MANY OTHER INTERACTIONS

These interactions don't usually count as small talk because you are only talking to them for a brief period like giving them your order or saying excuse me while passing by. However, once you master them, these mini-interactions *can* lead to small talk, if given the chance. Being able to hold your own in quick conversation can help you build confidence, make you more outgoing, and make you willing to engage in small talk.

So let's practice some micro-interactions.

Before we begin, let's do a brief check-in:

How comfortable do you feel about micro-interactions?

Please, don't look at me	○ 1	○ 2	○ 3	○ 4	○ 5	○ 6	○ 7	○ 8	○ 9	○ 10	I'm confident being in the world

Why do you feel this way?

....

....

....

....

....

....

What are you hoping to improve on?

....

....

....

....

....

....

Hello World! How to Talk to More People Daily

> **Small Talk Tip:**
> Keep in mind that your attitude informs everything. If you are positive and upbeat, more likely than not, people will be positive and friendly toward you. If you are anxious and feel awkward, people can also feel that energy. Keep it light! Keep it fun!

One of the most powerful words in any language is the word *hello*. It's simple, but it holds the power to connect us as people. It's why, when learning a new language, one of the first phrases you learn is how to say hello. It is more than just a greeting but a way of spreading kindness and building connections, even briefly. Even in our increasingly busy world when we rush to get in and out of places, it's important to make time to say hello to others to make them feel seen. While you don't have to stop and chat with them, for a moment you can make a connection, and that can feel pretty good.

COMMUNICATION CHALLENGE

Say hello to five strangers in one day. In the space below, write down who you said it to, what you noticed, and how it made you feel. Bonus points if you said this while smiling at them, nodding your head, or making eye contact.

....

....

....

....

....

....

....

....

....

....

....

....

Rate how it went:

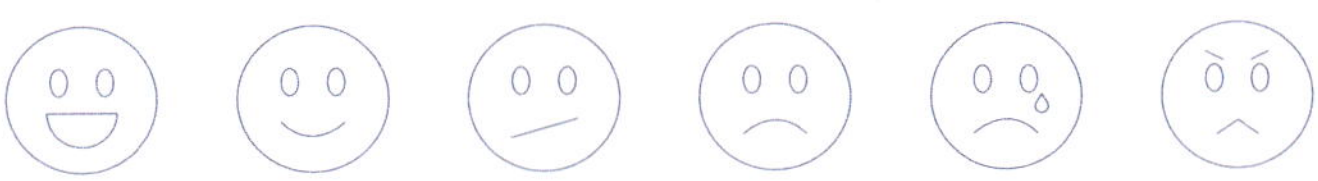

The Dos and Don'ts of Compliments

I *love* to give compliments. Ever since high school, I would be quick to give out a compliment while walking down the hallway, usually to compliment someone's outfit or shoes. Even in college, my friends often teased me for this, but why would I keep something nice to myself? I've gained a lot of friends and developed important relationships through my years of impulsive complimenting. But the biggest reward is seeing how much my compliments affect others. Whether it was a shy smile or their eyes lighting up, eager to chat, the two seconds it took to say something nice was worth it.

While giving a compliment can be an easy micro-interaction to practice, it's important to acknowledge that not all compliments are created equal or will be taken as compliments. Saying you like someone's shoes in the elevator is very different than screaming that you like someone's body out your car window as you pass by. So, let's take a little refresher course on the dos and don'ts of giving and receiving compliments.

DO

BE AUTHENTIC WITH YOUR COMPLIMENTS. If you truly like what someone is wearing or something they did, let them know with sincerity. "I loved your presentation on Friday. You really highlighted your points well."

BE SPECIFIC WITH YOUR COMPLIMENTS. Tell them exactly what you appreciate. "I love your outfit; the teal really makes it pop."

TRY TO KEEP IT NEUTRAL. Stick to things a person can control like their attitude, performance, or style.

BE GENEROUS WITH YOUR COMPLIMENTS. They're free!

ACCEPT THE COMPLIMENT THAT YOU ARE GIVEN. "Thank you so much!" is all you need to say.

DON'T

COMPLIMENT SOMEONE ON THEIR BODY, especially in the workplace or with people you don't know. You may have complimented someone on their toned arms without meaning anything by it, but it could come across as inappropriate.

GIVE OUT FAKE COMPLIMENTS. Don't compliment people for the sake of complimenting them, as you never want to come across as being phony. It could come back to haunt you.

GIVE A DIG AFTER A COMPLIMENT. "You look good for someone so short," is *not* a compliment.

PUT YOURSELF DOWN WHILE COMPLIMENTING SOMEONE ELSE. "Your hair looked so great today; mine is always a mess." Putting yourself down will not lift someone else up.

ARGUE WITH THE PERSON COMPLIMENTING YOU. We are often told to be modest and humble and downplay our good traits by saying, "Nah, it wasn't that good," or, "I think this makes me look ugly." However, this doesn't make you sound modest; it makes it seem like you lack confidence. Be bold: take the compliment.

FUN FACT:
Talking with people outside our social circle is considered so important that there's a National Week of Conversation in the U.S. and a National Conversation Week in the U.K.

What was the best compliment you've ever received, and how did it make you feel?

How do you react when someone compliments you? Do you tend to accept the compliment or deflect? Explain why you react that way.

CONVERSATION CHALLENGE

Over the next week, try complimenting at least 10 people about anything, from their haircut to their performance in a meeting. In the space below, write down your observations and record any compliments you received in return.

Rate how it went:

Mastering the Art of a Quick Chat

A quick chat is like small talk, but shorter. It's for when you're working on small talk with strangers but don't want to commit to a whole conversation yet. Quick chats can happen while checking out at the grocery store, going up on an elevator, or getting your mail. These conversations last for about a minute and don't get deeper than quick hellos and maybe a small comment on the weather or what's going on around you. Quick chats can lead up to small talk, but they can exist on their own.

While quick chats seem easy, they actually can be more intimidating than small talk, as you have so little time. Plus, it's easy to avoid them by looking at your phone or giving curt replies. However, learning how to chat quickly with the people around you can make you feel more confident and make the world seem a little less scary.

Here are the steps of a quick chat.

STEP 1

Open with a greeting. This can be as simple as "Hello" with a smile or nod, or mix it up with a "Good afternoon," "Happy Friday," etc. It's important to make eye contact, but don't stop what you're doing. If you're talking to someone who you're walking by, don't stop. Keep it moving.

STEP 2

Give a quick statement or ask a quick question that doesn't require a long response, something like: "How are you today?" "It's so nice outside." "I love your shoes." If you're moving, don't walk away from them before they can respond but keep your actions going. For example, if you're talking to a cashier, don't stop unloading your groceries, but don't leave until they answer you.

STEP 3

Say goodbye and end your conversation. This will happen naturally as one or both of you are leaving or your interaction is over. End the conversation with a "Have a nice day," or "Good seeing you," to end things on a friendly note.

That's the quick version of quickly chatting with someone. Don't worry; the more times you do it, the less you will overthink it.

Quick Chat Script

Let's look at how a quick chat can play out. Adam and Ben live in the same apartment building and are both taking the elevator.

ADAM: HEY, HOW'S IT GOING?

BEN: PRETTY GOOD, CAN'T COMPLAIN. YOU?

PRETTY WELL, IF IT WOULD STOP RAINING.

YEAH, THIS WEATHER HAS BEEN TERRIBLE. SUPPOSED TO CLEAR UP SOON.

I'M HOPING. TAKE IT EASY.

THANKS, YOU TOO.

CONVERSATION CHALLENGE

Within the next few days, try to have at least one quick chat with someone you meet out in the world. Record how it went here, including the time and place of the chat.

Rate how it went:

Mantras for Micro-Interactions

If you feel a little anxious about talking to people, even for a brief conversation, repeat these mantras to yourself before going out to help you build confidence and ease your anxieties.

I AM FRIENDLY AND APPROACHABLE.

SMALL ACTS OF KINDNESS NEVER GO TO WASTE.

I BRING CONFIDENCE TO EVERY WORD THAT I SPEAK.

I MAKE THE WORLD A BETTER PLACE WITH EACH SMALL ACTION.

THE COMPLIMENTS PEOPLE GIVE ME ARE TRUE AND COME FROM A GOOD PLACE.

Write down some other mantras that you can say or think to yourself to help inspire you.

....

....

....

....

CHAPTER CHALLENGE

Try out everything you learned in this chapter by having 10 micro-interactions with people in different settings. Record how it went below, including both highlights and things you could improve on for the next conversation.

Rate how it went:

Reflection Questions

What one piece of advice will you be taking away from this chapter? Write about how it has helped you or will help you.

Do you feel more confident about micro-interactions now than you were at the start of the book? Write why or why not.

USE THIS SPACE TO WRITE DOWN CONVERSATIONS YOU HAVE, JOURNAL HOW YOU'RE FEELING, OR HOW THIS CHAPTER HELPED YOU GET CLOSER TO YOUR GOALS. WHEN IN DOUBT, WRITE IT OUT!

“Conversation isn't about proving a point; true conversation is about going on a journey with the people you are speaking with.”

RICKY MAYE

CHAPTER 4

NEW AROUND HERE

Moving can be stressful, whether you're moving to a new city or a new country, going to a new school, or starting a new job. Not only are you in an unfamiliar setting, but you are also with unfamiliar people, which can make you feel nervous and lonely. Most people long for community, but it's difficult to build that when you feel like the odd one out. However, with the magic of small talk, you can work on building those connections, ease your anxiety, start feeling comfortable in your new setting, and begin to form a sense of community. Not only can that sense of community ease loneliness, but that familiar community can be there to offer help when you get into a jam.

So, let's take a tour around the world of friendly small talk in a new area.

Before we begin, let's do a brief check-in:

How comfortable do you feel making small talk in a new situation or location?

I FREEZE UP AND PANIC	○	○	○	○	○	○	○	○	○	○	I MAKE A GREAT FIRST IMPRESSION
	1	2	3	4	5	6	7	8	9	10	

Why do you feel this way?

....

....

....

....

....

....

What are you hoping to improve on?

....

....

....

....

....

....

Doing it Scared: The Importance of Putting Yourself Out There

I remember my first day at college. My parents helped me set up my dorm room, got me my books and student ID card, and said their goodbyes. The moment the door shut I had the terrifying realization that I was completely alone in a new place where I had to live for the next several months. I had some significant anxiety, and my thoughts started to race: What was I supposed to do now? What if I don't make any friends? What if everyone thinks I'm weird?

I decided then and there that the best defense is a good offense. Using a burst of nervous energy, I introduced myself to everyone on my floor. I figured this would be my only chance, as everyone was moving in—and thus, feeling the same level of nervousness and awkwardness as I was. I ended up meeting everyone on my floor, including their parents. I moved three people in (while wearing six-inch heels), and I showed a group of people around campus, despite only having been there for an hour. I was terrified the entire time.

But something amazing happened. As soon as it was over, I stopped feeling nervous. I made friends with some of the people I was sharing a building with and was at least on friendly terms with most people. I was familiar with the people coming and going from my building, which made me feel less anxious. Knowing my neighbors made it feel more like a home.

Since the "real world" obviously isn't confined to the relative safety of a college dorm, it can be a scary place, and it can be tempting to hide from people, as you don't know their intentions. However, you may find more peace by getting to know the people who surround your life. No one is an island.

When was the last time you did something that scared you? How did it go?

How well do you know your neighbors? Did you introduce yourself, or did they introduce themselves to you?

Won't You Be My Neighbor? How to Introduce Yourself

If you read that previous story and thought to yourself, "That's all well and good, but how do you introduce yourself to people without falling apart?" don't worry, we'll be going over it. Introducing yourself to your neighbors, whether you're new or they're new, can be nerve-wracking. Not only are you approaching them where you both live, but if the first meeting doesn't start on the right foot, it could lead to a lot of potential awkwardness down the road as you'll have to see this person so often. No pressure!

Seriously though, with a little confidence and the right tools, you can start making introductions and become at least friendly with your neighbors. Here are some tips on how to introduce yourself.

TIME IT RIGHT

It can be a little frustrating if you spent all that time building up the nerve and practicing what to say to your neighbor only to knock on their door and realize that they aren't home. A good way to prevent this is by first checking to see if their car is in the driveway or if they're outside or in the hallway (if you live in an apartment or dorm). If you're feeling bold, knock on their door, but if you're worried about intruding, wait until you see them hanging outside to make this introduction casual. Just don't wait outside their door or pounce when they first pull into the driveway, running over as soon as you see them, which could cause a little awkwardness.

SAY "HI!"

As mentioned in chapter 3, "hello" is a powerful word, ideal for breaking the ice with a new neighbor. Start with a friendly, enthusiastic greeting, followed by introducing yourself: "Hi! I'm Jenny. I live down the hall. I just moved in!" or "Hello, I'm John. I live in the yellow house over there. I noticed you're new and wanted to welcome you to the neighborhood." Easy as that!

DO A QUICK INTRODUCTION

One of the benefits of introducing yourself to your neighbors is that you can make some small talk without struggling to find a topic. On your first meeting, talk a bit about yourself without going into too many details. You don't want to talk their ear off about how you were born and raised in this town or that you moved into this building after your partner of six years broke up with you. Keep it brief at first by mentioning where you live and saying it's nice to meet them.

ASK NON-INVASIVE QUESTIONS

Yes, you're dying to ask about the best restaurants in the area or who's the best plumber to hire, but before you pick your neighbor's brain about everything, start by asking some simple questions, like how long they've lived here, whether they like it here, or how they are settling in. Don't ask questions like why they moved here, whether they live alone, or anything too personal yet. If they want you to know, they'll tell you.

DON'T BEGIN WITH COMPLAINTS

Keep your first introduction with your neighbor polite. You don't need to air any potential grievances on the first meeting like asking if their kids are loud and if they're always going to be playing their music at 3 in the morning. Remember, you have to live around these people, so keep it friendly.

DON'T OVERSTAY YOUR WELCOME

Your first introduction with your neighbors should be short, as you don't want to overstay your welcome. Wrap things up quickly and make plans to talk later if this chat goes well.

Small Talk Tip:

To gift or not to gift? It's commonly suggested to bring a gift—a tray of cookies, a potted plant, or a bottle of wine—with you when introducing yourself to your new neighbors as an attempt to break the ice. However, with people having allergies or preferences, you might want to forgo giving a welcome gift and just introduce yourself. If you'd like, consider bringing them a card or a gift card to a local store or restaurant if you're welcoming a new neighbor. You can also offer them assistance if they're moving in.

COMMUNICATION CHALLENGE

Introduce yourself to one of your neighbors. Bonus points if they just moved into your neighborhood. Record how it went below, including both highlights and things you could improve on for the next conversation.

Rate how it went:

New Friends in New Places

Moving to a new place can be a pretty lonely experience, especially if you're moving to an area where you have no connections or ties. There's also an additional challenge that it's much harder to make friends as an adult because we have fewer opportunities to socialize with new people outside of our daily routine: going to work, taking care of our children, taking care of ourselves.

However, you don't have to stay in isolation if you don't want to. Using your small talk basics, you may discover that a new setting is the perfect jumping-off point for making new friends. If you aren't sure where to start, here are a few tips to help get you out of your comfort zone and practice your small talk skills.

CHECK FOR EVENTS IN YOUR AREA

Even the smallest town seems to have something going on every week; you just have to look. Take a moment to look through your local community pages or online groups for events like meetups, outdoor concerts, craft fairs, hobby groups, farmers' markets, and other things you might be interested in. The benefit of these events is that you don't *have* to make small talk at first; you can just enjoy the event and work your way up to small talk.

TAKE A CLASS

Much like looking for local events, you can also find some classes to take in your area that align with your interests. Whether you're looking to take a cooking class or tap-dancing lessons, you can usually find something to fit your needs. Taking a class is excellent for making small talk because you already have something to talk about, making it easier to make conversation than trying to think up some causal topics.

DO VOLUNTEER WORK

Give back to your community while also becoming a part of it by doing some volunteer work in your area. Some great places to try are local animal shelters and food banks or helping clean up trails for local parks or nature preserves. If you have children, you can volunteer at their school to help at their events. Volunteering is a great way to make small talk and make friends, as you'll be around like-minded people who are also doing things they're passionate about. Remember, it truly takes a village.

GET INVOLVED IN YOUR COMMUNITY

In a similar vein, getting involved in your community could help you improve your small talk and make friends. This doesn't involve getting into your community's *business*, like gossiping about your neighbors or complaining loudly about everything, but getting involved in community events like going to town meetings, joining local organizations, and helping out when you can.

GO ONLINE

When single people move to a new place, one of the first things most of them do is log onto dating apps and start looking for matches. This is because society typically values romantic relationships more than platonic ones. It's easier to look for a date to show you around a new place.

However, online isn't just for dating anymore! Many apps are now catering to people who are looking to be "just friends" (yes, actually just friends). This is a great way to make new friends in the area, as these people are also looking for friendship, making small talk a little less awkward. (For advice on how to make small talk over text, check out chapter 8.)

COMMUNICATION CHALLENGE

Try one of the previous suggestions for activities, even if you aren't exactly "new" to your area. You don't *have* to make small talk your first time doing this, but you will get bonus points. Write about the experience below, what happened, what you enjoyed, and what you could do differently next time.

Rate how it went:

Small Talk Scavenger Hunt

In a 2022 study published in the *Journal of Experimental Social Psychology*, people reported avoiding small talk because they feared that the conversation would not go well. To ease this fear, the researchers had participants play a week-long scavenger hunt that involved talking to strangers. The results showed that people felt more optimistic about their conversation skills after the hunt, and they reported that the scavenger hunt was a positive experiment.

When moving to a new place, it can be hard to put yourself out there. So, here is a fun scavenger hunt, inspired by the study, to help you get out of your comfort zone and meet new people in your community. Now, you don't have to complete *all* of these in one week, but try your best to complete the scavenger hunt at your own pace. Don't forget to use the tips you learned in chapters 2 and 3 to navigate these conversations. You might be surprised at your results!

NOTE: Remember to use your best judgment during your scavenger hunt to keep yourself safe. Don't walk up to strangers that give you a bad vibe.

The Small Talk Scavenger Hunt

DATE STARTED: __ /__ /__ DATE COMPLETED: __ /__ /__

- ☐ Strike up a conversation with someone outdoors.
- ☐ Find your closest neighbor and talk to them for a couple minutes.
- ☐ Ask a server or barista how their day is going.
- ☐ Approach someone drinking coffee or tea and ask them what they recommend.
- ☐ Find someone wearing animal print and talk to them for a few minutes.
- ☐ Find someone who is wearing an accessory you like and compliment them.
- ☐ Find someone wearing a shirt with your favorite sports team/band and ask if they've been to a game/seen them live.
- ☐ Approach someone who has an interesting hairstyle or color and talk to them for a few minutes.
- ☐ Find someone eating a pastry and ask them if they'd recommend it.
- ☐ Talk to a person standing in front of you in line.
- ☐ Stop someone walking their dog and ask them a couple questions about the dog.
- ☐ Approach someone with a visible tattoo and ask them to tell you about it or where they got it done.

- ☐ Find someone who looks older than you and talk to them for a few minutes.
- ☐ Find someone who looks younger than you and talk to them for a couple minutes.
- ☐ Find someone with a manicure and ask where they got it done.
- ☐ Find someone wearing the same thing as you and compliment them.
- ☐ Stop someone wearing a watch and ask them for the time.
- ☐ Sit next to someone eating at the counter of your favorite diner and talk to them for a few minutes.
- ☐ Find someone sitting alone and talk to them for a couple minutes.
- ☐ Chat with someone in an elevator until you reach your floor.
- ☐ Find someone wearing a blue hat and talk to them for a few minutes.
- ☐ Find someone carrying a book and ask what they're reading.
- ☐ Approach someone you've seen around your community often and talk to them for a few minutes.
- ☐ Notice someone who is humming a song and ask them what the song is.
- ☐ Chat with someone who is indoors (waiting room, standing in line, browsing racks, etc.).

How do you feel after finishing the scavenger hunt? Were you nervous at the start of the hunt?

....

....

....

....

....

....

....

....

What was the hardest thing about the scavenger hunt? What was the easiest?

....

....

....

....

....

....

....

In what ways, if any, has your perspective or attitude on small talk changed after doing the scavenger hunt?

Write about one memorable conversation you had on the scavenger hunt. What did you gain from that experience?

Welcome to the Neighborhood Script

Now that we have an idea of how to meet your neighbors, let's look at it in action. Heather has just moved into the neighborhood, and Jill is eager to welcome her. Heather is carrying boxes into her house when Jill walks over to say hello.

JILL: HELLO THERE!

HEATHER: OH HI! I DIDN'T SEE YOU THERE.

WELCOME TO THE NEIGHBORHOOD! I'M JILL. I LIVE IN THE YELLOW HOUSE NEXT DOOR. I SAW THAT YOU WERE MOVING IN, AND I WANTED TO SAY HELLO.

OH, THAT CUTE HOUSE WITH THE LAWN GNOMES? I WAS JUST TELLING MY SONS HOW CUTE THEY ARE. I'M HEATHER, IT'S SO NICE TO MEET YOU.

OH, THANK YOU! MY SISTER GAVE THEM TO ME AS A BIRTHDAY GIFT. HOW'S THE MOVE GOING, HEATHER?

OH, PRETTY GOOD FOR THE MOST PART. I'M ORIGINALLY FROM NEW YORK SO THIS HAS BEEN AN ADJUSTMENT.

I TOTALLY UNDERSTAND. WE MOVED HERE A FEW YEARS AGO FROM SEATTLE FOR MY HUSBAND'S WORK AND IT TOOK A WHILE TO GET ADJUSTED. PLEASE LET ME KNOW IF YOU NEED ABSOLUTELY ANYTHING. I'D BE HAPPY TO SHOW YOU AROUND.

OH, I WOULD JUST LOVE THAT. THANK YOU SO MUCH.

OF COURSE! I'M HOSTING A PARTY AT MY PLACE ON FRIDAY. NOTHING BIG, JUST A BBQ WITH A FEW NEIGHBORS. I WOULD LOVE IT IF YOU WOULD COME WITH YOUR KIDS.

THAT'S SO KIND. THANK YOU SO MUCH. CAN I BRING ANYTHING?

JUST YOUR APPETITE! WELL, I WON'T KEEP YOU. BUT I'M RIGHT NEXT DOOR, SO IF YOU NEED ANYTHING, DON'T BE AFRAID TO HOLLER.

I WILL! IT WAS SO NICE TO MEET YOU, JILL.

YOU TOO!

Mantras for Social Interactions

If you're still feeling a little nervous about meeting your neighbors or moving around your community, try repeating these mantras before going out to help build your confidence. Remember, take it one word at a time.

THIS IS A NEW CHAPTER AND A FRESH START.

THE FIRST IMPRESSION I GIVE TO OTHERS WILL NOT MAKE OR BREAK ME.

I CAN FIND A COMMUNITY THAT ALLOWS ME TO THRIVE.

I AM LIKABLE AND PEOPLE WANT TO LIKE ME.

EVERYONE WAS THE NEW KID AT ONE TIME.

What are some other mantras you can say to yourself to help you when meeting people or when you're in a new situation? Write them here.

....

....

....

CHAPTER CHALLENGE

Try everything you learned in this chapter by making small talk with someone new to the neighborhood/building—or new to you. Write about how it went and include both highlights and things you could improve on for the next conversation.

Rate how it went:

Reflection Questions

When was your last major move? What was that experience like for you? Do you have any moves coming up in the future?

What is one piece of advice you will be taking away from this chapter? Write about how it has helped you or will help you.

Do you feel more confident about making small talk now? Write about why or why not.

USE THIS SPACE TO WRITE DOWN CONVERSATIONS YOU HAVE, JOURNAL HOW YOU'RE FEELING, OR HOW THIS CHAPTER HELPED YOU GET CLOSER TO YOUR GOALS. WHEN IN DOUBT, WRITE IT OUT!

> "Some of the most important conversations I've ever had occurred at my family's dinner table."

BOB EHRLICH

CHAPTER 5

AROUND THE TABLE

Ah, family. They're the people we love the most, but also the people who can drive us the most crazy—because they can. As we move from the kid's table to sit with the adults, there's a lot of adjustment. It's not just a holiday gathering anymore, whether you have to deal with nosy family members who ask invasive personal questions, get seated near those who only seem to want to argue with you, or be stuck in the room with relatives you barely know for hours at a time. There's a certain point in life when you realize that both you and your parents are adults, creating an interesting new dynamic to navigate that can be a little awkward.

Blood may be thicker than water, but it doesn't make it any easier to hold a conversation. In fact, it may be the familiar tension that causes so much awkwardness and unease. Fortunately, making small talk can help bridge the gap between staring silently at your plate and getting into a shouting match. And even if you get along great with your immediate family, there's bound to be a new or less-familiar person at the table at some point. While you may not achieve family harmony, you may be able to make it through dinner.

Before we begin, let's do a brief check-in:

How comfortable do you feel about family interactions?

CAN I GO BACK TO THE KID'S TABLE?	○ 1	○ 2	○ 3	○ 4	○ 5	○ 6	○ 7	○ 8	○ 9	○ 10	I TALK TO MY FAMILY ABOUT ANYTHING

Why do you feel this way?

....

....

....

....

....

....

What are you hoping to improve on?

....

....

....

....

....

....

Write a little about your family. Are you a big family? A small one? Close-knit, or don't see each other often? Write how you feel about this dynamic.

Who is the family member who's the easiest to talk to? Why is that?

Who is the family member who's the hardest to talk to? Why do you think that is?

Using Small Talk to Handle Family Events

Do you ever get a pit in your stomach whenever the holidays roll around? Maybe you dread the thought of attending family reunions or big family dinners so much that you try to find excuses to get out of them. It's not that you don't like your family, but it can be hard to talk to them and establish a connection with them. This could be especially true if you have a bigger family, or you're meeting with your partner's family. While being around people who are your family but feel like strangers can be an uncomfortable feeling, it doesn't have to be. Here are a few tips on how to navigate the situation with small talk.

GO IN WITH A POSITIVE ATTITUDE

Small talk is a mental game, and if you're in a good headspace, things will go a lot easier. Even if you're nervous about the family gathering, don't bring that tension in with you if you can help it. Go into it with a bright smile, an enthusiastic hello, and maybe some dessert, and you can tackle this situation with an optimistic mindset.

CONTROL THE NARRATIVE

If you get stressed out about what your family may ask you—for example, your job, your relationships, your personal life—it's a good idea to plan some stories in advance to talk about. A few days before the event, practice the subjects and the stories you want to tell your family. If you already have a topic in mind you wish to share, like a funny thing that happened at your job or the vacation you took, your family won't have to start digging for things to talk about with you.

THE BEST DEFENSE IS A GOOD OFFENSE

Another way to control the conversation is by asking questions. People want an opportunity to talk about themselves; they just want a way in. Instead of letting them ask the questions that put you in the hot seat, kick things off by asking a few of your own so they do most of the talking. Stick to easy questions that don't spark any hot-button issues. Here are a few examples to get you started:

I LOVE YOUR [INSERT ACCESSORY THEY'RE WEARING]. WHERE DID YOU GET THAT?

HAVE YOU BEEN ANYWHERE FUN RECENTLY?

HEY, REMEMBER THAT TIME WE [INSERT SHARED EXPERIENCE]?

YOUR POTATO SALAD WAS DELICIOUS. I'D LOVE TO GET THE RECIPE! WHERE DID YOU LEARN HOW TO MAKE IT?

These questions encourage people to tell stories and talk a little more about themselves.

BE A GOOD LISTENER

As always, being a good listener is key to successful small talk, especially where family is concerned, as some family members like to do most of the talking anyway. Make sure you make good eye contact, nod your head, and continue to ask questions to expand the conversation.

Small Talk Tip:

If you're at a family gathering, try to have a wing person with you, like a close sibling, cousin, or partner, to help you feel more at ease.

COMMUNICATION CHALLENGE

At the next family event, strike up a conversation with a relative you wish to get to know better. Write about how it went, including what went well and what you would improve on.

Rate how it went:

How to Turn an Awkward Conversation Around

Despite your best efforts, awkward conversations and uncomfortable moments are bound to happen at any family function. Whether they ask only inappropriate questions, or someone decides to go on a rant about the state of the world, you may be caught in the middle of a prickly situation. To avoid spending the rest of the evening hiding in the bathroom or storming out of the house altogether, here are a few tips to steer the conversation in a better direction.

PLAN YOUR RESPONSE AHEAD OF TIME

If you know someone is going to ask you an uncomfortable question or bring up a topic that is guaranteed to cause drama, try to have a prepared response so you don't get thrown off guard. You don't have to have a PR statement ready, but do have a response like, "I'm focusing on myself right now," or "I really don't know much about that. However, I did hear this interesting story about..." Be one step ahead of things.

CHANGE THE SUBJECT

At the end of the day, people prefer to talk more about themselves and what's going on in their personal lives than they do about your life or the state of the world. So, if someone starts asking about overly personal subjects, making offensive or inappropriate comments, or going on rants, bring the conversation back to them by asking questions. Asking your uncle about how his football team is doing will put him on a less-annoying tangent. Asking your cousin about her new poodle will take the heat off your love life.

DON'T TRY TO CHANGE SOMEONE'S MIND

More accurately: *Don't try to change someone's mind at the expense of your peace.* This is the most valuable lesson you can take with you when going to any family gathering. While you would love for your family to agree on every issue and always be thoughtful and empathetic to others, that doesn't always happen. As people grow more and more divided about issues, especially where politics are concerned, it's easy to get into a heated fight that could ruin the night.

With family, it's tempting to think that if you give a strong enough argument, you could win them over. This is rarely the case. If your mother hasn't changed her mind about something in over six decades, she's not going to change it because you yelled at her at dinner. In fact, debates can often strengthen people's resolve over their opinions, even if they only feel causally about it at first, because they are being challenged. Don't feed the trolls and remember it's okay to agree to disagree.

IT'S OKAY TO WALK AWAY

While this isn't to encourage you to pack up and leave because your family is saying something aggravating, don't force yourself to stay in a situation that is making you unhappy. It's perfectly okay to excuse yourself and go to the kitchen to help clean up or get seconds. Take it as an opportunity to calm yourself and allow the conversation to shift to a different topic in your absence.

Making the Connection: How to Reach Out to Family

> **FUN FACT:**
> If you pace while on the phone, psychologists think this may be a way to compensate for lack of non-verbal cues and body language you'd get in face-to-face conversation.

As we get older, our family relationships, whether by blood or by bond, become more and more important. Whether we become nostalgic about our past or need people to lean on as we move into the future, it truly does take a village. It doesn't matter if you're interested in reaching out to a cousin you never really talked to at family gatherings but always thought was cool, or you're looking to strengthen your relationship with your sibling—it can be hard to take the first step. You may feel awkward or do not know how to make the first move. Fortunately, small talk can help. Here are some tips to keep in mind when building these connections.

MAKE THE FIRST MOVE

If you want to build a relationship with someone, family or otherwise, don't wait around for them to come to you. Reach out to them either by walking up to them at the next family event or messaging them on social media. Start by saying "hi" and go from there; remember, you're not talking to a total stranger.

SHARE STORIES, NOT GOSSIP

As mentioned, swapping stories is a good way to build connections without getting too deep. If you remember a story about the person you're talking to, ask if they remember, too, as that can be a conversational jumping-off point. Saying things like, "Hey, remember when Dad took us to the lake, and we saw that huge fish?" or "I was thinking about you recently! I found that T-shirt in my closet we got from our trip to Boston," are conversation starters that can spark connection. Make sure these stories are positive to the other person; don't bring up sad or embarrassing stories. Keep it light.

KEEP EXPECTATIONS LOW

While small talk can achieve a lot of things, it usually doesn't transform your relationships from distant to extremely close in one conversation. Don't assume that your great aunt is going to leave you something in her will because you said you liked her hat. Keep your expectations for your first conversation low so you don't put too much pressure on yourself.

CONTINUE TO BUILD

Small talk is an excellent building block, but make sure you keep working on those conversations. Continue to make small talk as you build up your relationship to deeper conversation and connections. The more you do it, the more comfortable you'll feel.

Learning from Our Loved Ones through Small Talk

It's important to build connections with your family, as they may not always be around to talk to. Don't let your fears of making a little awkward small talk keep you from learning more about the people you love; you may not always get these opportunities. Even if your grandmother is intimidating, you might regret that you didn't learn more about her life while she was here. Or maybe a parent has a secret technique for making perfect roast chicken or a unique way of staking garden plants. Ask them about it now!

What are you most afraid of when talking to your family? Write down some fears and possible ways to counter those fears below.

CONVERSATION CHALLENGE

Before you make small talk with one of your older relatives, ask if you can record it on your phone. Not only can you hear yourself making small talk and see where you may need to improve, but you'll also have a voice recording of your loved ones while they're with you. Who knows? You may have recorded an enlightening conversation you'll treasure forever. Write down your thoughts about your conversation below.

....

....

....

....

....

....

....

....

....

....

Rate how it went:

Family Small Talk Script

Let's look at how small talk with a family member can play out. At the annual family summer cookout, Michelle runs into her Aunt Martha, whom she hasn't seen since the holidays.

AUNT MARTHA: MICHELLE? IS THAT YOU? HOW ARE YOU, DARLING?

MICHELLE: AUNT MARTHA! IT'S SO LOVELY TO SEE YOU! I LOVE THAT BROOCH YOU'RE WEARING.

OH THIS OLD THING? I'VE HAD IT FOR AGES. YOUR UNCLE ALBERT GAVE IT TO ME FOR MY BIRTHDAY WAY BACK WHEN.

WELL, IT'S SO CHARMING.
I KNOW YOU HAVE A THING FOR FROGS.

OH YES, EVER SINCE I WAS A KID, THEY HAVE BEEN MY GOOD LUCK CHARM. HEY, WHERE'S THAT BOYFRIEND OF YOURS? NO WEDDING BELLS YET?

OH, HE COULDN'T MAKE IT. SO,
FROGS ARE YOUR GOOD LUCK CHARM? WHY?

WELL, WHEN YOUR MOTHER AND I WERE LITTLE, WE WOULD GO TO THIS LITTLE LAKE EVERY SUMMER AND—ACTUALLY, THIS IS A REALLY FUNNY STORY, LET ME START FROM THE BEGINNING.

I'D LOVE TO HEAR IT.

Mantras for Family Communication

If you're still feeling anxious about your next big family event, take a moment before you walk in to take a deep breath and repeat these mantras. They may help keep you sane if there's some family drama.

I'M HERE TO ENJOY THE MOMENT.

I CHOOSE TO LISTEN WITH EMPATHY AND COMPASSION.

MY PEACE IS MORE IMPORTANT THAN SOMEONE ELSE'S OPINION.

EVERYONE'S FAMILY IS A LITTLE WEIRD.

EVERYONE IS DOING THEIR BEST.

What are some mantras you can say to yourself to bring you confidence when talking to your family? Write them here.

....

....

....

....

CHAPTER CHALLENGE

At the next family gathering, try to talk to at least five family members that you haven't really spoken to before—and don't forget, kids count! Record how it went below, including both highlights and things you could improve on for the next conversation.

Rate how it went:

CHAPTER CHALLENGE

Sit down next to a family member that you don't know too well or rarely see at a family dinner and make small talk with them throughout the meal. Record how the conversation went and what you learned about them.

Rate how it went:

Reflection Questions

What one piece of advice will you be taking away from this chapter? Write about how it has helped you or will help you.

....

....

....

....

....

....

Do you feel more confident about making small talk with your family now than you were at the start of the book? Write about why or why not.

....

....

....

....

....

....

....

USE THIS SPACE TO WRITE DOWN CONVERSATIONS YOU HAVE, JOURNAL HOW YOU'RE FEELING, OR HOW THIS CHAPTER HELPED YOU GET CLOSER TO YOUR GOALS. WHEN IN DOUBT, WRITE IT OUT!

> *"Ultimately, the bond of all companionship, whether in marriage or friendship, is conversation."*

OSCAR WILDE

CHAPTER 6

FOR THE LOVE OF SMALL TALK

"Hey, are you a library book? Because I'm checking you out."

Cheesy pick-up lines aside, dating can be a nerve-wracking experience for some. If you want a grand romantic love story, you're going to have to go through a lot of first dates, which means making small talk. There's nothing worse than planning a date, getting ready for it, showing up, and realizing you have nothing to say to this person. It's awkward enough to make you want to log off dating apps.

Fortunately, dating doesn't have to mean that you struggle to make conversation. Mastering the art of small talk can help make dating easier. While not every first date will lead to a lasting romantic relationship, it will make every date more comfortable and even fun. While this book won't be teaching you the best pick-up lines or how to have a successful relationship, it will go over the ways that "small talks" can be the building blocks for a successful relationship.

Before we begin, let's do a brief check-in:

How confident do you feel making small talk on a date?

CLAMMY JUST THINKING ABOUT IT	○	○	○	○	○	○	○	○	○	○	NATURAL FLIRT
	1	2	3	4	5	6	7	8	9	10	

Why do you feel this way?

....

....

....

....

....

....

What are you hoping to improve on?

....

....

....

....

....

....

....

What was the best first date you've ever been on? Write about what was so memorable about it and why you enjoyed it.

What was the worst first date you've ever been on? Write about what went wrong and how it made you feel.

What is the most intimidating part about going on a date for you?

How to Break the Ice on a First Date

First dates can be riddled with anxiety. Whether you met this person on a dating app or you've asked out someone you've known for a while, a first date could be the start of something new; and that can add a lot of pressure. This is much different than normal small talk because regular small talk has lower stakes. We aren't hoping to build a sense of intimacy and a meaningful relationship with our rideshare driver or the cashier at the grocery store. With dating, we are hoping to build a deeper connection with someone else, which could lead to nerves and overthinking.

However, there's no need to panic. Here are some easy tips to break the ice on a first date.

PICK A SETTING YOU'RE COMFORTABLE WITH

A dinner and a movie is a classic first date idea, but that doesn't mean you *have* to do it. In fact, a dinner and movie can be even more nerve-wracking because you're expected to have dinner with someone you barely know, then sit in silence with them for two hours in the dark. If you're planning the date, try to find a setting that makes you more comfortable, like going to your favorite book shop or out for milkshakes. First date activities like bowling or apple picking or ice skating can break some of the tension by having you both doing something active while (hopefully) talking to each other.

START WITH A COMPLIMENT

It's always good to start with a compliment when going on a date, as it makes the other person feel good and can lead to conversation. Saying that you like their shirt could lead to a conversation about where they got it, while complimenting them on how they are on-time can show them that's a quality you value. Either way, a compliment starts the date on a positive note. (Flip back to page 62 if you need a refresher.)

DON'T MAKE IT FEEL LIKE AN INTERVIEW

It's easy to start asking rapid-fire questions of your date about their life: What do you do for a living? Where are you from? Do you have children? What's your five-year plan? What do you like to do for fun? These are all good questions, but don't ask them all in a row like it's a job interview. It's important to let the conversation breathe and see where it takes you naturally. Here are some easy conversation starters; pick one or two of these questions to get started.

WHY DID YOU PICK THIS RESTAURANT?

HOW WAS YOUR DAY?

DID YOU ALWAYS LIVE IN THIS AREA?

WHAT WAS THE LAST TV SHOW YOU WATCHED IN ONE SITTING?

WHAT DO YOU LIKE TO DO IN YOUR SPARE TIME?

WHAT ARE YOU READING?

DON'T GIVE ONE-WORD ANSWERS

There's nothing worse than going on a first date and all your date replies with are one-word answers: "yes," "no," "accountant," "Baltimore." It really kills the mood and makes it harder to spark conversation. Lead by example and answer any question you receive with a thoughtful answer. You don't have to give your who life story, but try to open it up to conversation.

MY DAY WAS GOOD, BUT THE WILDEST THING HAPPENED ON MY WAY OVER HERE. I WAS DRIVING TO THE RESTAURANT WHEN A CHICKEN *LITERALLY* CROSSED THE ROAD. AND HE WAS JAYWALKING!

I WORK AT A LITTLE BAKERY DOWNTOWN. I'M CURRENTLY TRYING TO SAVE MONEY TO GO TO PASTRY SCHOOL. DO YOU HAVE A FAVORITE DESSERT?

I ACTUALLY GREW UP IN A LITTLE TOWN IN NEW YORK AND MOVED HERE A FEW MONTHS AGO. ARE YOU FROM AROUND HERE?

ASK QUESTIONS THAT GIVE YOU A GLIMPSE INTO THEIR LIFE

While you don't want to ask about marriage or how many kids they want and potential baby names on the first date (or at least, don't make it your first questions), you can learn a lot about a person by asking simple questions that can help you get an idea about their life and see if their values align with yours.

DO YOU HAVE A FAVORITE MOTTO THAT YOU LIVE BY?

ARE YOU A DOG PERSON OR A CAT PERSON?

HOW WOULD YOU DESCRIBE YOUR PERFECT DAY?

WOULD YOU DESCRIBE YOURSELF AS AN IDEALIST, A PESSIMIST, OR A REALIST?

ARE YOU AN EARLY BIRD OR A NIGHT OWL?

Most of these questions seem simple, but they can lead to some interesting conversations that can tell you a lot about the person.

TALK ABOUT WHAT YOU'RE LOOKING FOR

While a first date isn't the best time to be planning your wedding, it's important to be open and upfront about what you're ultimately looking for. A mistake that most people make is trying to be nonchalant about their intentions to not sound desperate. However, if you're someone who is dating to ultimately get married, you don't want to waste your time with someone who's just dating for fun—and vice versa. Be honest about what you're looking for to avoid hurt feelings and wasting everyone's time. You can still have a fun first date without having to go anywhere further.

Small Talk Tip:

If you're anxious about meeting someone for the first time on a date, break the tension by calling them on the phone or using a video chat. This gives you a way to "meet" the person and get to know them a little bit before the date. If things don't click during the phone call, you can always cancel the date.

EMBRACE THE AWKWARD SILENCE

Even the most talkative person deals with awkward silences on a date, especially a first one. Awkward silences happen, so instead of feeling uncomfortable about them, embrace them. If you're going to be dating someone for the long haul, there's going to be silence at times, so this is a good way to tell how someone can handle quiet moments. If the silence goes on for too long, you can always crack a joke to break the tension.

KEEP IT SHORT (AT FIRST)

Some of my best first dates lasted for hours, but that doesn't mean they started out like that. When planning a first date, keep the itinerary simple with an activity that doesn't take a lot of time, like going out for coffee or getting ice cream. If the date goes well, coffee can turn into getting lunch or ice cream can lead to going for a walk in the park. If you don't have chemistry with the other person, you can finish your coffee and say goodbye. No pressure!

CONVERSATION CHALLENGE

Before your next first date, write down five questions you want to ask on your date to break the ice. Practice them a few times before the actual date begins. Afterward, record how they went over.

Rate how it went:

How to Tell if Someone Is Flirting with You

One of the most challenging things about learning how to make small talk is trying to tell the difference between when someone is flirting with you or if they're just trying to make small talk. All the social cues—making eye contact, compliments, open body language—are similar. However, there are a few key differences between flirting and being friendly that can help you navigate the dating world. Here are a few ways to tell if someone is flirting with you and how to flirt with others:

- MAINTAINING EYE CONTACT FOR LONGER THAN USUAL, OR FREQUENTLY LOOKING AT YOU, EVEN IF THEY'RE TALKING TO SOMEONE ELSE
- MAKING JOKES AND LIGHTLY TEASING YOU
- LAUGHING AT YOUR JOKES, EVEN IF THEY'RE NOT FUNNY
- MIRRORING YOUR GESTURES AND BODY LANGUAGE
- TOUCHING/PLAYING WITH THEIR HAIR
- BITING OR LICKING THEIR LIPS
- LEANING IN WHEN YOU TALK
- LIGHT PHYSICAL CONTACT: TOUCHING YOUR ARM, FEELING THE MATERIAL OF YOUR JACKET, BUMPING SHOULDERS, ETC.
- FINDING REASONS TO STAY AROUND YOU, EVEN AFTER THE CONVERSATION HAS ENDED
- MENTIONS SEEING YOU AGAIN IN THE FUTURE

CONVERSATION CHALLENGE

Look out for the signs on the previous page the next time you are making small talk with someone to see if they're flirting with you. Do you consider yourself a flirt? Do other people call you a flirt even if you don't realize you're doing it? Write about a flirtation experience below.

Rate how it went:

Using Small Talk in Established Romantic Relationships

So you made it past the first date, and you've developed a solid relationship; that's the end of small talk, right? WRONG! In fact, small talk becomes more important the longer we've been with someone. Life can get hectic with bills to pay, work stress, and children to take care of; it's easy for couples to stop talking to each other when getting lost in their own life. In fact, some couples can get into the "roommate" phase of their relationship when they only talk about what needs to be done around the house or their schedules. Without conversation, even the strongest couples can lose their spark. How can you get it back? Through small talk, of course. Here are some ways to use small talk in your relationship.

MAKE THE TIME

When life gets busy, it's easy to put your relationship on the back burner, especially when you have children or demanding jobs. But no matter how chaotic life gets, take a few moments to talk to your partner and give them your full attention. That means putting your phone away, turning off the TV, and sitting down and looking at them so they know they have your full attention.

KEEP IT LIGHT AND FUN

This isn't the time to talk about how they didn't put their shoes away or that they need to call the repair man about the gutters. Those conversations can happen later. For small talk, try to keep it easy. Ask them about the book they're reading, something interesting that happened at work, or what you're hoping to do together this summer.

Allow this to be a moment where you're just happy to talk to each other.

ALLOW IT TO SINK INTO DEEPER CONVERSATION

Small talk can be a gateway to deeper conversations, so continue to ask questions and be an active listener during your talk. It could help you learn more about your partner and bring you closer together.

MAKE SURE SMALL TALK ISN'T YOUR ONLY TALK

Small talk is a great way to connect with your partner, but if all you talk about is the weather or basic household management, you may have communication problems in your relationship that will require a deeper conversation.

First Date Script

Let's look at how a first date conversation could go. Riley and Chris met on a dating app a week ago and decided to meet at a coffeeshop on a Saturday afternoon.

RILEY: CHRIS?

CHRIS: RILEY? HI, IT'S SO NICE TO MEET YOU!

NICE TO MEET YOU TOO. I REMEMBER ON YOUR PROFILE THAT YOU ARE A COFFEE SNOB, SO I HOPE THIS PLACE MEASURES UP.

THIS IS ACTUALLY MY FAVORITE COFFEESHOP IN TOWN. THEIR LAVENDER LATTES ARE TOP TIERED.

NO KIDDING! I COME HERE EVERY FRIDAY. THEIR ALMOND SCONES ARE THE BEST IN THE CITY.

TRULY! I'VE BEEN TRYING TO RECREATE THEM AT HOME.

OH, YOU'RE A BAKER. YOU MIGHT BE WINNING MY HEART OVER ALREADY.

AN AMATEUR BAKER AT BEST, HAHA. ALMOST BURNED MY KITCHEN DOWN MAKING BOXED CAKE MIX.

HAHA, OH EVERYONE HAS AN OFF DAY!

OH, YOU'RE TOO KIND. I LOVE YOUR WATCH, BY THE WAY.

THANK YOU! MY DAD GAVE IT TO ME WHEN I GRADUATED COLLEGE A FEW YEARS AGO.

ARE YOU CLOSE TO YOUR DAD?

OH YEAH, WE'RE A VERY TIGHT-KNIT GROUP. BIG FAMILY DINNERS EVERY SUNDAY. ARE YOU CLOSE WITH YOUR FAMILY?

VERY! I HAVE FOUR SIBLINGS AND WE'RE ALWAYS IN EACH OTHER'S BUSINESS—FOR BETTER OR WORSE.

HAHA, I'LL STAY ON MY TOES. HEY, ARE YOU GETTING HUNGRY? THERE'S A LITTLE PLACE DOWN THE STREET THAT HAS THE BEST THAI FOOD.

I'D LOVE THAT.

CONVERSATION CHALLENGE

Try making small talk with a person you have known for a long time and are close with. This doesn't have to be a romantic partner; you can also do this with your best friend or a parent. Record how it went and what you may want to improve on next time.

....

....

....

....

....

....

....

....

....

....

....

Rate how it went:

Mantras for a First Date

First dates can make even the most social person anxious. To ease your first date jitters, here are some mantras to repeat to yourself before your date.

I'M BRAVE FOR PUTTING MYSELF OUT THERE.

I TRUST MY INTUITION.

IT'S JUST A DATE.

THEY'RE JUST AS NERVOUS AS I AM.

I AM WORTHY OF LOVE.

What are some mantras you can say to yourself to hype yourself up before a big date? Write them here.

....

....

....

....

....

....

CHAPTER CHALLENGE

Using everything you learned in this chapter, ask someone out on a date. You can do this! If they say yes, write about the date and how it went. Did you do any flirting? Is there anything that could have been improved on?

Rate how it went:

Reflection Questions

What one piece of advice will you be taking away from this chapter? Write about how it has helped you or will help you.

....

....

....

....

....

....

Do you feel more confident about dating and flirting now than you were at the start of the book? Write why or why not.

....

....

....

....

....

....

....

....

> "A single conversation across the table with a wise man is better than ten years mere study of books."

HENRY WADSWORTH LONGFELLOW

CHAPTER 7

PROFESSIONAL SMALL TALK

Office culture has changed dramatically over the last few years. Gone are the days when we would chitchat around the water cooler; now we're sending emojis over Slack channels or trying to work the camera on video calls. If you find yourself going back to working in an in-person, on-site environment, or find yourself in a new hybrid situation, it might be intimidating working face-to-face with people again; you can't simply mute your audio or turn off your camera when you don't want to interact. You're going to have to make some small talk along with doing the tasks you get paid for. (And even in an entirely remote situation, you'll still need to make small talk when you check in with your supervisor or when you write an email to a colleague—see chapter 8 for more on that.)

While this may sound like a drag, it can actually be beneficial. For one thing, small talk can certainly make the workday go by faster. You don't have to make your coworkers your family, but you are going to be working with them for eight to twelve hours a day for four or five days a week, so you should at least make it a tolerable experience. Being in the office also gives you a chance to connect with higher ups that could help you get promoted or find opportunities for career growth. Whether you love it or hate it, small talk can give you an edge in your career. You just need to find the right words.

Before we begin, let's do a brief check-in:

How comfortable do you feel about making small talk in the workplace?

THIS CHAPTER COULD HAVE BEEN AN EMAIL	○	○	○	○	○	○	○	○	○	○	I LOVE CHATTING WHILE GETTING COFFEE
	1	2	3	4	5	6	7	8	9	10	

Why do you feel this way?

....

....

....

....

....

What are you hoping to improve on?

....

....

....

....

....

....

What kind of job do you have? How important are conversation skills to that job?

Have you ever (or ever felt like) you missed out on a big opportunity or job because of your conversation skills? Write about the situation and what you think went wrong.

How to Use Small Talk in Job Interviews

Every stage of looking for employment can be stressful. First you need to comb through hundreds of job postings, fill out numerous applications, write individual cover letters, and then be interviewed multiple times—all just to go to work! Though an interview is the final stage of the job-hunting process, it's the most crucial. While you may sound good on paper, meeting someone in person can help the hirer decide if you're right for the job and the company. They want to see that you can do the thing you promised on your resume, but also if you are personally a good fit. That's where small talk comes into play.

You may be thinking. "That's not fair! I have everything they're looking for on the application and they won't hire me if they don't think I'll fit in because I don't make small talk?" And you're right, it's not fair. However, it's important to remember that communication is a soft skill: an interpersonal skill that applies to any profession and is based on how you interact with others. Being able to communicate well is an important skill to have—even essential to some careers. While you may not need great communication skills to be an engineer, it's hard to be a salesperson without them.

It also comes back to company culture. You are spending a solid chunk of your week with these people. While someone's work performance and experience may be perfect, if they're a bit of a jerk, the whole team suffers.

Fortunately, there are easy ways to make small talk in interviews without sounding phony.

Small Talk Tip:

It sounds simple, but smiling can help people feel more at ease and give them a good first impression of you. While you don't have to smile the whole time, giving a smile when you first enter the interview can really help you win people over. Plus, it can make you look more confident.

BE POSITIVE AND ENTHUSIASTIC

Even if you're nervous about your interview, try to walk in with a positive attitude. The interviewer wants to see that you're excited about the position and eager to get started, not someone sitting there bored waiting for this to be over. Start off by saying hello, that you're happy to meet them, and chat about the work you've done and the work you want to do. If they see that you're interested in the work, they'll be interested in you.

COMMENT ON SOMETHING RELATED TO THE COMPANY

You should always do your research about the place you're interviewing for. Much like in dating, the interviewer knows that you've been looking at other jobs, but they want to feel special, that you really want to be with them. Mentioning something you learned about the company or the company culture (how you admire their value statement, enjoyed a recent ad campaign, heard about their lunchtime walking club, etc.) can help you stand out from other candidates. It can also lead to more discussion about the company, which can help you make the decision of whether you want to work there.

KEEP IT PROFESSIONAL

During an interview, it's okay to talk about your interests, your hobbies, where you went to school, and things of that nature. In fact, it could help you bond with your interviewer if you share a common interest. However, be sure to keep it professional. Don't bring up personal things like your messy divorce, or that you've been trying to get pregnant, or this is the tenth interview you've been on this month—it may hurt you more than it helps.

ASK QUESTIONS

Never leave an interview without asking at least one question. Not only does asking questions help you learn about the job and the company, but it also tells the interviewer that you are interested in the position. Here are some good questions to ask:

HOW IS SUCCESS MEASURED IN THIS ROLE?

IS THERE ANYTHING IN MY RESUME YOU WERE CURIOUS ABOUT?

WHAT WOULD YOU SAY THE CULTURE IS LIKE AT THIS COMPANY?

WHAT IS YOUR BEST DAY ON THE JOB?

What was the best interview you've ever had? Write about what went well.

What was the worst job interview you ever had? What went wrong, and what could you improve?

CONVERSATION CHALLENGE

Preform a mock job interview with a friend and have them score you on how well you did. Afterward, have a conversation with them about what they thought were your strengths and weaknesses, and write down their observations.

Rate how it went:

How to Make Small Talk in a Professional Setting

So, you got the job. Does the small talk end? Nope! In fact, you probably have to engage in even more small talk now that you're employed. Especially if you work in an office. Whether you need to talk to the receptionist, see people chatting in the break room while having lunch, ride the elevator to the fortieth floor, or attend an office party or picnic, the need for small talk is everywhere. By learning to master it, however, you can make better professional connections and build bonds that can help you career-wise and mentally. After all, most people don't want to spend their whole workday in complete silence. Here are some tips on how to yap at the office.

OBSERVE OTHERS' COMMUNICATION STYLES

You don't have to bring your small talk game just yet. Take a few moments to observe how your coworkers communicate with each other. Do they joke around a lot? Do they usually talk by the coffee machine? Do they talk about TV shows? Knowing how small talk works in the office can help you plan your own strategy.

JUST JUMP IN

If you hear a group of coworkers talking about your favorite movie, don't be afraid to jump in with your opinion, if it fits the topic. This is easier than trying to get small talk going by yourself and makes you feel included in the group. However, make sure this is a public conversation. If you see people talking with each other off to the side, don't butt in.

SHARE SOMETHING SMALL, BUT PERSONAL

While you shouldn't give your coworkers your life story, sharing something personal about yourself can help you connect with them. Talking about your tomato garden or showing pictures of your pug can help you make small talk and make you more memorable.

BRING IT BACK TO WORK

Small talk is just that, small. A few conversations during your break are fine, but don't let someone take up your work time by talking your ear off. Don't be afraid to say, "Well, I better go finish my report. It was fun chatting with you," and leave it at that.

CONVERSATION CHALLENGE

Listen to a non-private conversation at work and get a feel for how they talk and the topics they discuss. Then, join the conversation if you feel comfortable. Write about it here. What are some takeaways that you observed? Bonus points: Within the next two weeks, start a conversation at work.

....

....

....

....

....

....

....

....

....

....

....

Rate how it went:

How to Network

FUN FACT:
The average person speaks around 16,000 words per day.

It's all about who you know. While training and degrees are nice, being able to network and connect with people is how a lot of opportunities are given and received. Employers are more likely to hire people they know, or who have been recommended by people they know, than a stranger. Networking can also help you meet new clients and even make a sale. Even if you're a shy wallflower or you're entirely happy at work, you should make an effort to network; you never know where it may lead you. Fortunately, there are ways to make the process less painful.

MAKE THE FIRST MOVE

It's important to remember that everyone is nervous at a networking event. Even the person who's shmoozing everyone in the room was terrified at one point. So be bold and introduce yourself to people. They'll be relieved that someone is speaking to them instead of standing there awkwardly. To ease the tension, bring business cards with you as an opener.

BE GENUINE

A good part of this book talks about the importance of being enthusiastic and giving out compliments when making small talk. While this is true, it's just as important to be genuine with people. Try not to overwhelm people with a lot of over-the-top compliments and flattery like they're being sold something. A simple "It's nice to meet you" or "I read your recent article; it was very well written" can get you far.

BUILD RAPPORT

When it comes to networking, it's important to find common ground so you have something to build on when making a connection. Maybe you both went to the same graduate school or you both play pickleball; finding that thread of connection can help make you memorable and allows small talk to flow with ease.

TALK ABOUT GOALS

The point of networking is to find people who you can build a professional relationship with. Therefore, it's important to share interest in what they want to achieve and if you can help them with that goal. Maybe the person you're talking to wants to develop a stronger brand and you just so happen to have worked on three successful brand campaigns. While they may not be able to use you now, they at least know about your skills and goals.

WRAP IT UP WITH PLANS TO FOLLOW UP

There are usually a lot of people to talk to at networking events, so try to keep the conversation moving to not waste anyone's time. When possible, hand out business cards with your contact information so you can talk again later.

CONVERSATION CHALLENGE

Go through your local events calendar or emails and look for three networking events in your area. These could be happy-hour events, conferences, or job fairs. Attend one and write about how it went.

Rate how it went:

Job Interview Script

Now that we know what to do when making small talk in a professional setting, let's see it in action. Chloe is applying for an editor position at a publishing company and is being interviewed by Sophia. Here is the first part of the interview.

SOPHIA: CHLOE MAXWELL? COME ON IN.

CHLOE: IT'S SO NICE TO MEET YOU, MRS. ALEXANDER.

OH CALL ME SOPHIE. PLEASE, SIT DOWN.

THANK YOU. YOU HAVE A LOVELY OFFICE. I LOVE YOUR DESK.

OH THANKS. IT'S A LITTLE CLUTTERED, BUT THAT'S HOW I LIKE IT. SO, ARE YOU FAMILIAR WITH OUR COMPANY?

OH YES, I'VE READ SO MANY BOOKS BY THIS PUBLISHER. I JUST FINISHED READING YOUR LATEST RELEASE AND I COULDN'T PUT IT DOWN. BUT MY FAVORITE IS *THE ALCHEMY* THAT YOU PUBLISHED A FEW YEARS BACK.

OH THAT'S ONE OF MY FAVORITES TOO. WE GET A LOT OF GREAT TALENT HERE.

I BET YOU DO. I WOULD LOVE TO HELP YOU FIND MORE OF IT.

Mantras for Professional Small Talk

Whether you're going in for a job interview or going back to the office after time off-site, here are some mantras to repeat to yourself before going in.

I HAVE THE COURAGE TO SEIZE ANY OPPORTUNITY THAT COMES MY WAY.

MY BEST IS GOOD ENOUGH.

I AM RESOURCEFUL AND CONFIDENT.

PEOPLE WANT TO LIKE ME AND WORK WITH ME.

MY TALENTS SPEAK FOR THEMSELVES; MY WORDS JUST GUIDE THEM.

What are some mantras you can say to yourself to get ready for a job interview or going back to the office? Write them here.

....

....

....

....

....

CHAPTER CHALLENGE

Using what you learned in this chapter, find three professional events where you can make small talk. This can be at the office, at a job interview, or during a networking event. Record how they went below, including both highlights and things you could improve on for the next conversation.

Rate how it went:

Reflection Questions

What is one piece of advice you will be taking away from this chapter? Write about how it has helped you or will help you.

Do you feel more confident about professional interactions now than you were at the start of the book? Write why or why not.

USE THIS SPACE TO WRITE DOWN CONVERSATIONS YOU HAVE, JOURNAL HOW YOU'RE FEELING, OR HOW THIS CHAPTER HELPED YOU GET CLOSER TO YOUR GOALS. WHEN IN DOUBT, WRITE IT OUT!

"Almost all good writing begins with terrible first efforts. You need to start somewhere."

ANNE LAMOTT

CHAPTER 8

WRITTEN COMMUNICATION

Throughout this book, we have discussed the importance of verbal communication. Written communication, however, is also important to the art of small talk—especially as we are having more and more conversations online, from writing a friendly email to sending texts and DMs. While we may not consider small talk to take place in a written format, our online life is built around creating conversation, from writing work emails that help you build a relationship with clients and coworkers, to texting people in a parenting group to get to know them.

As with verbal communication, making small talk in written communication has its strengths and weaknesses. With written communication, you don't have to focus on body language or social cues that can be misread. You can also communicate with different methods like emojis or GIFs to get your point across. However, because you don't have body language cues or can't hear someone's tone, it's much easier to miscommunicate over text. Without seeing the person, especially someone we don't know very well, we can overthink word choices and what we "think" they mean, or pore over their use of punctuation to see if they are actually upset with us. Autocorrect also creates miscommunication that wouldn't happen with verbal communication, so written communication has some pros and cons.

Whether you're text savvy or you've just started using your email, here's how to develop small talk in writing and online.

Before we begin, let's do a brief check-in:

How well do you communicate through writing?

WHAT IS A GIF?	○	○	○	○	○	○	○	○	○	○	I'D RATHER TEXT THAN TALK
	1	2	3	4	5	6	7	8	9	10	

Why do you feel this way?

What are you hoping to improve on?

How to Make Small Talk in the Digital World

In chapter 2, we discussed the basic steps of small talk. However, those four steps don't transfer as easily when writing a text or email. Things like body language or tone of voice no longer matter because you're not having this conversation verbally, in-person. And you kind of have to be on your phone if you're communicating on your phone. The general steps of small talk, however, still apply; they just look a little different.

STEP 1

BE PRESENT

How does one be present through texting? By responding in real time. It's a pain to be texting someone back and forth and then not hearing from them for several hours in the middle of the conversation. If you're trying to make small talk through text, make sure you are focused on the conversation. Don't be playing a game or scrolling through social media or cooking dinner. This doesn't mean putting your life on hold until the conversation is over, but make sure you are staying up to date on your conversation. (And if you must leave or pause the conversation, simply tell them.)

STEP 2

ASK OPEN-ENDED QUESTIONS

Fortunately, this step is the same for verbal communication. In fact, this step may be easier in writing, as you might feel more comfortable asking these questions without feeling nervous or afraid you are taking up their time. You can also ask more questions since you don't feel you have a time limit like in-person conversation. Make sure you limit yourself, however, as you don't want to pepper someone with questions all night.

STEP 3

READ CAREFULLY

While you can't usually listen over text (unless your phone reads your texts to you), reading your text carefully is similar to being a good listener. It's important to read texts closely, not just keep texting the other person anew without first replying to their messages. You can even show that you're "listening" by liking their messages with emojis.

Small Talk Tip:

Texting is a very different style of writing than email or even writing a letter. For example, grammar is usually ignored, a period at the end of the sentence means you're being serious, using "K" as a quick response might actually make people think you're mad at them, and typing in all caps with exclamation points means YOU'RE EXCITED, NOT MAD!!! Acronyms are still popular, with more being created each year. If you aren't sure what an acronym means, look it up before using.

STEP 4

RESPOND ENTHUSIASTICALLY

This step is even more important in written communication because it shows that we are "listening" to what the other person is saying. Typing one-word answers or even a single letter, like "K" (rather than "OK"), might give someone the wrong idea about your feelings, even if you aren't actually feeling that way. Similar to verbal communication, respond to what the person is saying with follow-up questions and opinions. You can also use emojis, memes, and GIFs to get your point across. However, make sure these are appropriate for the context of the conversation. Sending a meme to someone you matched with online is fine; sending it to your boss may be crossing a line. Use your best judgment.

When did you first start texting? How old were you? How has texting changed since you first started?

How has texting affected the way you communicate daily?

Who are the people you text the most? What do you talk about?

COMMUNICATION CHALLENGE

Text someone you don't often text and start making "small talk" with them; see how far you get in your conversation. Use the space below to write how it went and what you learned from it.

Rate how it went:

How to Write a Professional Email with Small Talk

With more work being done remotely, writing professional emails has become more important than ever, whether you are looking to get a job or trying to build a better relationship with a client. Emails are often more formal than text messages, but it's not the same as writing an actual letter. You can still have fun and make small talk while keeping it professional onscreen. Let's go over how to write a professional email for any situation.

INTRODUCTION

Remember, this is not a letter. You don't have to start off with "Dear, —." You can start by saying "Hello, [insert name]" or "Hi, [insert name]!" which comes off as a little more friendly while still being professional. However, make sure you greet them by their name, not just saying "Hi!" or "What's up?" If this is your first time emailing them and they don't recognize your username, start by telling them who you are and where they know you from.

FIRST PARAGRAPH

The first part of your email is considered the "small talk" part. You can ask how they are doing, if they are doing well, and some small tidbit or light question. Usually, people write emails to ask specific questions or gain more information, so you can keep this part of the email light. Here's an example on the top of the next page:

SECOND PARAGRAPH AND BEYOND

If you're sending an email to ask about something, share information, or offer something, this is where you would put it. For example, if you were emailing Julie about the upcoming class field trip or a business idea that you had, this is where you would write about it.

FINAL PARAGRAPH

End your email by going back into small talk mode, whether you ask them what they think, ask them to connect with you later, or even just wish them well. Then add your sign-off and signature and you have an email. Remember, this isn't like writing a letter; you can still be professional *and* casual.

COMMUNICATION CHALLENGE

Practice your email writing skills by creating a few drafts of an email and sending them to yourself. These can be real emails you wish to send at a later date or made-up situations. Do about three drafts and write your favorite below.

Rate how it went:

Texting Script

Let's look at how small talk through texting can play out. Nikki and Ian are in the same chemistry class and recently found each other on social media. They are now chatting through a messenger app.

Mantras for Written Communication

While written communication may not seem as nerve-wracking as verbal small talk, here are some things to keep in mind that can build your confidence and help you not overanalyze every text you send or receive.

I AM CONFIDENT IN MY ABILITY TO GET MY MESSAGE ACROSS.

PEOPLE READ MY MESSAGES WITH THE BEST OF INTENTIONS.

I HAVE THE TIME AND THE CLARITY TO WRITE. I DON'T NEED TO RUSH MY REPLY.

I KNOW HOW TO EXPRESS MYSELF BEST.

I ENJOY COMMUNICATING WITH PEOPLE IN ALL FORMS.

What are some mantras you can say to yourself before texting? Write them here.

....

....

....

....

CHAPTER CHALLENGE

Pull out your phone and scroll through your contacts. At random, message five people and start a conversation with them. See how far you get with your small talk. Use the space below to record what happened.

Rate how it went:

CHAPTER CHALLENGE

Review some of your texts or emails where a miscommunication happened. In the space below, write about what you think went wrong and how you would fix it now. Go ahead and rewrite those texts below, fixing them. Bonus points if you text that person, talk about your mistake, and try to fix it.

Rate how it went:

Reflection Questions

How has written communication changed the way you perform small talk with others?

....

....

....

....

....

....

What is one piece of advice you will be taking away from this chapter? Write about how it has helped you or will help you.

....

....

....

....

....

....

....

....

Do you feel more confident about written communication now than you were at the start of the book? Write why or why not.

USE THIS SPACE TO WRITE DOWN CONVERSATIONS YOU HAVE, JOURNAL HOW YOU'RE FEELING, OR HOW THIS CHAPTER HELPED YOU GET CLOSER TO YOUR GOALS. WHEN IN DOUBT, WRITE IT OUT!

Afterword

GOODBYE AND GOOD LUCK

WELL, IT'S TIME TO END OUR LITTLE CONVERSATION. I HOPE YOU ENJOYED IT JUST AS MUCH AS I DID. BUT THIS ISN'T GOING TO BE THE ONLY CONVERSATION YOU'LL HAVE. INSTEAD, IT'S THE STARTING POINT ON YOUR JOURNEY TO MAKING MORE SMALL TALKS, AND MAKING YOU FRIENDLIER, CONFIDENT, AND READY TO TAKE ON THE WORLD. BEFORE WE SAY GOODBYE, HOWEVER, LET'S DISCUSS HOW YOU'RE FEELING.

Do you feel more confident about your small talk abilities now than before you started the book? Write about why or why not.

What do you feel like you most improved on when making conversation?

What is left for you to improve on?

Think a little bit about the goals you wrote at the start of the book. Have you achieved any of them yet? Have they changed?

NOW, GET OUT THERE AND GET CHATTING!

References

Fenning, Chris. *The First Minute: How to Start Conversations That Get Results*, Alignment Group, 2020.

Fine, Debra. *The Fine Art of Small Talk: How to Start a Conversation, Keep It Going, Build Networking Skills—and Leave a Positive Impression!* Rev. ed. Hachette, 2023.

Jardim, Carla. "The Big Deal about Small Talk." *Family Practice Management*. 2004;11(9):68.

Jenkins, Richard. "British People Will Spend over Four Months of Their Lives Talking about the Weather, Study Says." *The Independent* online, August 2018.

King, Patrick. *Better Small Talk: Talk to Anyone, Avoid Awkwardness, Generate Deep Conversations, and Make Real Friends*, Independently published, 2020.

Martino, J., J. Pegg, and E.P. Frates. "The Connection Prescription: Using the Power of Social Interactions and the Deep Desire for Connectedness to Empower Health and Wellness." *American Journal of Lifestyle Medicine*. 2015 Oct 7;11(6):466-475.

Mehl, Matthias R., et al. "Are Women Really More Talkative Than Men?" *Science*. 2007 Jul 6;317(5834):82.

Popomaronis, Tom. "You Know Those People Who Pace While on the Phone? Science Says They Have It Right, After All." *Inc.* online, August 23, 2016.

Sanstrom, Gloria, Erica J. Boothly, and Gus Cooney. "Taking to Strangers: A week-long intervention reduces psychological barriers to social connection." *Journal of Experimental Social Sociology*. Sept 2022;102(11).

Shapira, Allison. "Why Fillers Words Like 'Um' and 'Ah' Are Actually Useful. *Harvard Business Review* online, August 2019.

Ward, Adrian F. "The Neuroscience of Everybody's Favorite Topic." *Scientific American* online, July 2013.